Affection for the Unknowable

Greg,

For our efforts to find the words for what is beyond words.

Sam

Affection for the Unknowable

Poems by

Len Anderson

Hummingbird Press
Santa Cruz, California

Library of Congress Control Number: 2003110184
ISBN: 0-9716373-5-0

Acknowledgement is gratefully made to the following publications,
in the pages of which many of these poems first appeared:
Bellowing Ark, "Monday Morning." *PoetsAgainstTheWar.org*,
"Another One," "Where We Are Headed." *Quarry West, Poets and
Writers of the Monterey Bay,* "Wauna." *Sand Hill Review*, "Anchor,"
"Nail Clippings Are Rich in Nitrogen," "Reason for Amnesia." *Santa
Cruz Sentinel*, "Why Dervishes Whirl" as "Why Dervishes Turn."
Sarasota Review of Poetry, "Ghazal with Black Hat" as "Black Hat
Poem." *Something Like Homesickness*, "Cots," "Excerpt from the
Obituary of a Postmodernist Critic," "It's Better to Be Depressed
Than Watch TV," "Today I Am the Summer Grass." *The Dallas
Review*, "Holy Cross Junior Prom." *The DMQ Review*, "Morning
Ghazal," "Night Ghazal," "Open Ghazal." *The Montserrat Review*,
"Angel in a Cage," "Breakfast with My Father at Two AM," "Kinship
with Silence" as "Sonance," "My Father's Prayer," "The Spiritual Life."

The author would like to thank the following individuals for their
encouragement and help with these poems and this book: Richard
Maxwell, Robert Bly, Kathy Abelson, Terry Adams, Mary-Marcia
Casoly, Elizabeth Biller Chapman, David Cummings, Christine
Holland, Meredith Ittner, Muriel Karr, Jackie Marderosian, Jim
Standish, Eve Sutton, Louise Whitney, Marcia Adams, Virgil Banks,
Dane Cervine, Jenny D'Angelo, Guarionex Delgado, Kathleen
Flowers, Kate Hitt, Carol Housner, Ted Kagy, Robin Lopez Lysne,
Phyllis Mayfield, Maggie Paul, Stuart Presley, Joan Safajek, Lisa
Simon, Robin Straub, Philip Wagner, Joan Zimmerman, Julia
Alter, Jonell Jel'enedra, George Lober, Joanna Martin, Tilly Shaw,
Debra Spencer, Tamara Wagner, Ken Weisner, Elke Maus, and
especially Joseph Stroud and Joseph McNeilly.

Design and layout assistance: Kate Martini.
Cover art: Ken Conklin.
Section Title Page art by Joseph McNeilly and Len Anderson.
Photo of the author by Joseph McNeilly.

Hummingbird Press
2299 Mattison Lane
Santa Cruz, CA 95062-1821

Printed in Canada

Contents

Animal Is Spiritual

To my wife Elke

who feeds me.

Physics is mathematical not because we know so much about the physical world, but because we know so little: it is only its mathematical properties that we can discover.
—Bertrand Russell

Man can embody truth but he cannot know it.
—William Butler Yeats

Kinship with Silence

Affection for the Unknowable

Let's chop down the beanstalk climbing into the sky of *I Am Sure*.
Let's roast the Giant in the holy fires of doubt and make our song *We
   Are Not Sure*.

At age seven I lived in the presence of God. When the priest
asked me to confess my sins, I could only answer, *I'm not sure.*

How many souls burn in the flames of war
because a few men are not man enough to say, *I am not sure?*

In ninth grade algebra I took as my guru, *X*. I follow still
its first teaching: *To know me, say first, I'm not sure.*

Aquinas had it all wrong: our language must describe the world, not
the world conform to language. To be human is to hang on the cross,
   ever unsure.

Every atom in the universe is a quantum cloud of doubt.
God must really like *I'm not sure's.*

A friend asks, *Why drag God into your poems?* Early in life I grew fond
of the unknowable. And one of the names of God is *I'm not sure.*

We speak and the tongue trembles; we sing, the whole body quakes.
All the libraries in the world add up to *I'm not sure.*

It's scary how quiet Len can be: his whole body fixed,
breathing stilled, eyes turned down, deep in another *I'm not sure.*

The Spiritual Life

At age three I looked out the living room window,
saw faces glow in the night.

And climbed the winding stairs,
gazed out the window halfway up,
saw the night sky open before me,
felt the ocean inside me open.

At seven, asleep, I swear
a man entered my room, touched my foot;
I screamed as one about to die.
My parents searched the room,
the house, found no one.

Father Lawrence came to our parish, led us in song,
walked up and down the aisle praising God
and us. We all joined in, our voices—my own voice—
filled the church, reached heaven.

I thought if God would call my name
as my mother did
when dinner was on the table,
then I would know God was real and I
was His son or a chosen one.

During Mass at school I fainted
and Sister Mary Helen dragged me out to the fresh air.

One summer day a friend and I lay back on the grass,
saw sky, a few thin clouds,
and I asked, *When I die what will I become,*
blue air, white clouds?

At age thirteen, I began to pleasure myself;
it was a sin;
sometimes I confessed it and sometimes not
and that was a sin
and I did not confess that sin,
and finally I confessed all,
said my penance of rosaries,
masturbated again,
didn't know if I would go to Heaven
or Hell.

I went to the church, wanted to go behind
the altar, find God hiding there,
but knew already,
knew the priest and his sadness.

I tried the new sacraments,
marijuana, LSD,
looked for God in them, found myself
and my own sadness. Tried yoga
and meditation,
sought peace and found longing,
sought wisdom and found
I needed to become human.

I fell in love with a woman. Once while making love
a white fireball of kundalini
rose up my spine, melted in my brain.

I have worked hard, become a success, a man,
whatever that is. Now I wonder
what I am, why
I am so afraid.

A friend tells me we are God, we are Light. I
live in the edge of the shadow
of a thing so huge I cannot see—staying at the edge
I neither freeze nor melt.

He tells me again, we
are all pieces of God. I
am a broken bowl,
with drops of that ocean
I felt as a child still on me,
glistening.

And now I wake at three AM, find
these words turning in me;
I turn with them, wrestle
for hours with a dark wraith
till exhausted we collapse
together in mute joy
for just one breath,
then struggle on.

Cots

Los Altos in the fifties
was an apricot orchard
with houses snaking in. We
lived the rhythm of twenty-two trees:
Blossoms like snow
set our saliva to rise
until July when we could eat
the first high, red-cheeked ones
right off the branch,
scoop the fallen soft ones gently,
perhaps even wash a few
if Mama was around.

When we were full,
we'd cut and strip a springy branch
and make a cot-apult: Slit a cot,
squeeze out the pit,
impale on the branch and whip
to fling it out of sight,
splat on somebody's car. In fall
we'd rake the leaves in a pile,
fall into it and die,
spring back to life, screaming.

My first job was picking cots;
I had a crush on a cutter
named Andrea Leonard;
I figured it was fate—
our names contained each other. She
didn't think much of me,
still soft and fuzzy as an apricot.

After all these years I'm still crazy
about cots,
so my wife and I got a tree. Now
I split one open,
pop half of heaven in. Nectar

swirls in my mouth and I'm
fourteen, at the top of the ladder,
sun in my eyes, muscles aching.
I strip a long branch of ripe fruit,
top off my bucket,
scramble down the ladder,
lug it to the crates,
tumble them gently in;
Old Frank punches my ticket,
and I'm an eighteen-cent
richer man.

Reason for Amnesia

I forget why the smell of pool chlorine
made me want to skinny-dip,
which, of course, I never did—Aunt Mayme
would have come out and asked me
what the hell I was doing.

I forget if it was June or September—
Newell and I set up a high-jump bar;
he sailed over easily and I did, too; well,
almost, and we heard Gail and Linda
next door behind the fence, giggling.

I forget if it was
the Temptations or Little Richard
I dreamt played on my radio all night
and wouldn't turn off,
even when I turned the knob
hard to the left, pulled out the plug,
certain my parents could hear.

I forget how that stone looked,
why Newell and I picked it up,
smashed it open,
saw the vein of red
running from a solid red heart,
why we made a stone bleed.

And I forget
which girls I wanted to dance with
at the Saturday Stomp, but could not ask
because I would have to talk with them
and then
all the blood in my body
would rush up
through my throat into my head
and I would die.

Today I Am the Summer Grass

on a hillside where I played
with Newell and Spud
one day when I was sixteen.

How we loved
the easy power of gravity
as we pried loose and rolled
boulders down the hill, how we loved
the gathering speed, the rumble,
then the tearing through the chaparral, the shattering
of madrone and scrub oak, the crack
of stone on stone.

And the one we rolled the other way,
that lumbered down,
then sped and leapt over the road
inches above the one car
passing.

How I ran for years.

Holy Cross Junior Prom

I used to go to sock hops,
but I never asked girls to proms—
I didn't know who I liked. Charlene
must have liked me. She
was tall and as skinny as I, but a brunette,
while I had blue eyes,
blonde hair held with Brylcreem
and a few big pimples. Her skin was clear.
She wasn't really pretty, but the main thing was
she was nice and she asked me, so I went.

My father drove; at the door
she introduced me to her father
as *Larry*, I told her
Leonard, she apologized
and introduced me again.

I really can't remember her dress.

I think the gym looked fine.
They had tables with four chairs
so two couples could sit and talk
and a stage with the band.

The nuns were nice and didn't bother us much.
We sat at the table some and stood some.
I wonder what we talked about;
probably our teachers and stuff.

The band was good. It was rock 'n roll
when it still had the roll. The guy
on the saxophone was great.
The big thing then was the Twist;
we probably danced every one of them.

I remember best the slow
dances. We would huddle close,
try to hold our arms right,
step and sway a bit with the rhythm,
and turn now and then
so it wouldn't get too boring.

I liked it best when my
groin would brush her,
or sometimes I would even
hold it against her for a little while.

I wondered what she felt.
I didn't want her to think I was bad.
If I started to get hard,
I would back off a bit.

I suppose all this was sort of training
for later years.

On the way back, I let her out of the car
and said goodbye on the sidewalk.

The next day my mother asked
if anything went wrong.
I said, *No, it was fine.*
And I called Charlene
just like my mother said to,
and thanked her
and told her I had a good time.

She said she liked the corsage.

The Way Through

Inside the log, cells explode, boil and rise to feed the flame.
And we two feed ourselves into the flame.

On my knees by the water heater, I tend a match to its open throat
and wonder if my prayers will be answered with a flame.

My father was Norwegian, my mother Catholic—
I've spent many years making sure not to burst into flame.

I light a candle to remember: I am part bee,
part clover, part soil, part sky, and all flame.

I told her I'd like to check out our thermochemistry.
Turned out she was oxygen, I was fuel, I went up, then down,
     in flames.

Friends, when you run into a burning house to save a child,
the only way through the fire is to become flame.

Breakfast with My Father at Two AM

The day after Christmas, after ninety-one years,
the timer in his heart gave out.
My mother called for an ambulance
and doctors put a small box in his chest,
fed wires through veins to his heart,
and made it beat.

Even hooked to tubes and wires,
he tried to get out of bed,
so my mother stayed one night.
But the nurses asked her to leave
and called a cab.

The next night it was my turn.
By ten o'clock I was tired
and turned out the light. But he
needed to talk. He,
who held his words back, confided
the last three years had been hell,
my mother obsessed
that another woman
would steal him away.

I began to understand those phone calls:
she would call and tell me
she was leaving,
but wouldn't say why.

And how the day before
she awoke in the night,
didn't know who or where she was,
dialed 911;
a policeman came, told her her name,
said she would be fine in the morning.

So I assured my father
it was not her fault.
Perhaps her brain was getting old.
He said maybe his was, too.

Then, at two AM
he announced
it was time to make breakfast.
I told him where we were
and for a moment
he seemed embarrassed.
Then he asked
if I would like a frozen waffle
and there in the dark
dropped one into a toaster
only he could see,
poured coffee, lifted a cup,
savored the brew. I,
who have always loathed
frozen waffles and coffee,
said yes, and in the dark cave
of the hospital room,
I took the broken bread
he offered me,
I held the cup to my lips.

My Father's Prayer

Ninety-two, half bound, half gagged by stroke,
back home in a hospital bed,
he commanded the physical therapist to go,
and called for the priest, who absolved him
with the names of the three
I never knew he believed in.

Facing the dark chasm,
he began his prayer
to his mother, twelve brothers and sisters
gone ahead, and to God: *Oh help me, I
have lived by the rules,
was never a drunkard or cheat.*

Four days and nights he called out,
I am ready,
and every hour, Death's tailor,
Apnea, fitted his new suit,
helped him try it on,
shut his eyes, stopped his breath
one eternal minute,
till he climbed out, gulped in air,
took up again his song
of ecstasy and terror.

When I, at the chasm of day, of night,
step back in fear,
I hear my father's prayer
and stumble ahead. I gasp, I cry,
yet come to sing,
I lurch, yet cross.
I hear my father
but one step
before me.

Angel in a Cage

Where is my husband?
my mother asks,
a week after his funeral.
   There is no such thing as eggs,
she says, as I set down the plate,
   There is no such thing as breakfast,
and begins eating.

Helping her walk to his grave
I hear the click of bone on bone
in her knee. Later she tells friends,
   Today in the cemetery
   there was the marker
   with Andy's name and mine.
   They're all ready for me.
   If I get tired of it here,
   I can go there and move in.

When my wife pays a visit,
my mother tries to shut her up,
then leaves burners on;
a pan melts and bursts into flame.

We hire a live-in companion. My mother,
who has never spanked us,
slaps her, tells her,
   You do not know
   how to water the lawn,
storms out to inspect it,
turns back, screams,
   Now you've locked me out.
   Let me in! Let me in!
breaks the window with her fist.

At lunch she tells me
I think I'm not the same person.
Someone else pushes their way in.

Every week I do the shopping,
take her to lunch, for rides.
Once she proudly tells me,
You've come a long way.
You carry your own weight and more.
The next day,
You're not my son, you're my bodyguard.
If I recognized you as my son, I
would slit my throat.
I yell, "I am your son! I am your son!"
hug her and cry and wonder
who I am hugging.

After six months
in the hospital bed in her room,
she stops eating. The live-in caregiver
asks why.
Because I am dead.
I've been dead three days.
The caregiver holds the mirror to her face,
tells her she is very much alive.
She eats again.

Late one afternoon the sun
streams around the curtains
into her room. She asks me,
How much is there to that angel?

I look around and ask, "What angel?"
    That one in the cage,
she tells me, pointing to the fan
where I see three wings.
I say, "Oh, this one
who keeps you cool on hot afternoons,"
and turn it on.
We hear the flutter.
We feel the breeze from its wings.

Kinship with Silence

The meadow and the round hills have waited all night
for this: The dew falls. The dew rises.

I have been apprenticed with Norwegian masters—
If you can't say it with silence, it isn't worth saying.

Once I just had to tell the truth,
now I'm grateful for even a word.

I mold these sounds with delicate care,
all to record my own bursting.

I can't go to the big church anymore—
I got caught using the wrong metaphor.

Sometimes, all alone, I listen
to the stillness rolling in in dark waves.

Dying can be a lot like being born:
We don't know the name of the one we cry out to.

The Average Moment Is Two Seconds Long

The speckled spider
and the web that runs
from the fuchsia out to the persimmon tree
are beautiful for days
till a sudden gust of wind
rips one strand
and the web is gone. After a long
work day, the business page
of the newspaper
plants one foot firm
in the center of my chest
and boots me away. My wife,
in the middle of cooking dinner,
says, *I'm so tired I forget to breathe,
I could scream!* Then the wind settles down
and the spider is out on a leaf
spinning from its body
one long line
it will ride again on the wind
out to that tree.

As a Child I Would Practice

jumping, spend hours,
aim for the tops of trees,
pause at the peak, float
and lose myself
in the trance of the fluttering leaves
and the migrating geese
that cross the sky,

until the day
I had no wings,

and fell
for the longest time
past the darker leaves,
and thickening branches
my spell unraveling,
each year gathering weight

until the arms of the earth caught me.

Now and then I take to the air again
and I have no idea which
I love more:
the sky that opens out
with tree-top tender leaves,
or the solid trunk,
the earth that yet holds me.

Spring

and my wife is in the garden
planting pole beans, pod peas,
blackberries, basil, zucchini and chard.
Everything survived our second winter here—
hundreds of succulents sit fat and happy.
The apricot and Santa Rosa plum,
the Fuyu persimmon, nectarine
and cherry are starting to look like trees. She
brings carloads of straw for mulch,
sings praise to each of her earthworms.

Beauty can only stand being hidden so long: See
how the honeysuckle, daisies and sage
break into bloom, see the white butterflies,
painted ladies. Now she finds a gold bug,
cousin of the ladybug, but gold
as a ring and more rare.
She sets out a lid for garter snakes to hide under,
tips it one day to find two entwined.

Tonight our salad of dandelion, arugula, cilantro,
Persian mint, lemon balm, parsley and dill.
We are promised tomatoes in sixty-four days
and the orange and lemon are bearing, too.

Some say this is the time before
eternity—we work so hard to wake up. But see
how the earth wheels
a few more degrees about the sun,
and golden poppies
spring up all around us.

From the House of Amphibian Song

When I forget to sing, it is a sad day.
When I remember
it is still a sad day, but at least I sing.

Each winter I mourn the passing of the green tree frogs
who lived in the field next door
before the tractors and houses came.

(I can do this without a thought
of the ones who lived here on this land
under my own home.)

Oh, when I walked out into the field,
stood stock still
as their thousands of voices filled the air.

Such changelings! I've seen them go
from green to grey to brown
to pure transparent
here in the warmth of my own hand.

And where are the garter snakes that fed on them,
where the hawk and kestrel?

Their song flowed from the pond and the green field,
mine whistles from the hollow
made by their loss.

Tonight I sing for us all.

The Painter
for Ken Conklin

Because I asked him to, my friend Ken
sits on the grass at 8:19 on a Saturday morning
in front of a mound of rock and soil and plants
with easel and palette and tubes of paint,
bends over a spiral rosette of the succulent,
Echeveria Afterglow, to fully see the light
that emanates from the pinkish edges of its thick,
bell-shaped, magenta and lavender leaves,
then leans back to his palette to mix
this unnameable tint and place one dab
on the canvas just so, because soon
it won't be 8:19 any more,
the hues will have changed, the shadows shifted.

Of course he has picked this plant for its light,
but also because I asked him to,
because my wife and his
are deeply enamored of succulents,
these survivor plants that I swear
came from another planet,
not just because of this eerie light,
but also the way they infiltrate everywhere,
and their quiet charisma, which leads my wife
to walk through the garden saying
This is my favorite of one, and
This is my favorite all the way down the row
as she has also said of the nape of my neck
and all down my shoulder and chest
because that glow is everywhere, is
in all its forms unnameable
and leads us to do
extravagant things. Just look at Ken,
bent over *Echeveria Afterglow:* He
has painted for forty years
and hung paintings everywhere in the house,
all for that glow, to live
in its radiance.

For the Record

One morning my mother awoke
and didn't know who she was,
or where, or how she got there.
She was eighty-three, at home alone,
my father in the hospital.
All she could think to do
was call the police.

And now I hear on the radio,
it is true: Our sense of self
is built and housed here
in the right frontal lobe
and can vanish as quickly
as the keys to your car.

One day it will be too late,
so I will tell you now:

I am this pair of red-tailed hawks
wheeling above, his love-screech
circling with them,
her legs and talons extended.

I am the ocean waves
that wrap around my legs,
then roll out again.

I am everyone I love
and most,
my wife Elke
with whom I delight
to live out
each day.

Night Ghazal

My love and I and the golden poppies sleep beneath the wing of
   the night
and this deep field of stars is also covered by the night.

I catch sight of her beauty and she asks, *So who do you love?*
Only you, I answer, only day, only night.

In our sleep the redwood tree and I trade dreams:
It flies an airplane; I am borne by dark winds through the night.

The frogs and crickets and I know one another well;
we hear each other's love calls late in the night.

All day I work hard to pay off my debts;
one just grows deeper—my debt to the night.

Sages tell us to prepare for death. I say,
I'm doing all I can—I practice as I fall asleep each night.

To Serve the Lame God

Listen, Hephaestus

You, whose feet were crushed
when you were cast out of heaven
and struck this Earth,
yet chose to fashion armor
and thrones for the gods
from deep in your volcano,
I wonder
if you fashioned me.

Do you recall
the crystal radio you helped me build
on the workbench in the garage,
and the telephone wires we strung
to Scott's house, walking the fence,
the dogs yapping and clawing beneath us?
How he and I had nothing to say
over those wires,
but that didn't matter,
we had made our own telephone;
that was enough.

Do you recall
how soft I was, how easily formed?

❄

I did not see, but you
were always there
as I bent over a circuit board
and struggled to trace the paths
of electrons. Now
I feel you here
in every piece of metal
extruded or bent. I feel you in me,
for I am not only human,
I am also a telephone pole,

antenna for the cosmic
microwave background,
ganglion of nerves, wires and optic fibers
that cross the sky and ocean floor. My thoughts
are on every tongue;
I do not own my thoughts,
my nerves, Hephaestus.
Do you hear them there
in your volcano, as I do in mine,
that hum and crackle of voices?
Do you wonder as I do,
Is my own heart
my own heart?

Before I was optical fiber,
I was the iron you heated,
pounded and bent, and I was the flame,
your hammer, too. I was the ore
in the mountain, the wolf,
his call in the night, and the moon. Now
I am a spool of cable,
eight hundred sixty-four strands of glass.
I will run from land to land,
carry our voices, faces,
do your magic. Look how the spider
spins a web from her own body—
surely there is no crime in that.

Yet, here is our gift and curse:
you and I are not well bonded
to either Heaven or this Earth,
and bend matter to our own will.
In shaping
we are shaped, too,
are bent and walk this Earth
dragging malformed limbs.

Listen, Hephaestus,
today I renew the ancient rite
with tools you vested in me—
diagonal cutters, laser, blowtorch—
to open, burn and cut you apart
and eat each nerve, muscle and bone,
as every living thing is consumed
so others may live.
I feed all who hear me
that they may know
you
are ever among us.

The Birds in the Bevatron

Eight years in grad school is one way to say *forever*
and thirty-eight hours up on the hill
at the Berkeley Rad Lab in my experiment shack
going back and forth over walls of racks of NIM electronics,
checking, tuning, debugging, and finally taking data
is another. The oscilloscope flashes
the arrival of another squirt of carbon nuclei careening
through the maze of magnets at almost the speed of light
into our paraffin target. The Nixie counter
lights up the toll of spattered nuclei and I'm punch drunk,
need to go before I mess up bad.

I update my cheery colleagues and manage
somehow to let go of it all and get out the door.
I'm heading across the Bevatron floor when I hear,
above the gentle whirr of fans, the chug of vacuum pumps,
and the ramping hum and cutoff of accelerator magnets,
a bird
warbling in its nest up on top of the concrete blocks
that absorb the warm bath of neutrons
from the accelerator walls and beam dumps.
I'm so tired, I, too, could nest right here
on the concrete floor and go to sleep,
but I wonder where these birds
think they are, here inside the Bevatron,
no green in sight, and don't they know
it's after midnight—the only light
from rows of fluorescent tubes and the whirling red
lamp of warning.

They must be as crazy as I am
to seek shelter here—I
who am driven by some
madcap desire to understand, to be here
at the moment of creation, logbook in hand
with spectrometer, arrays of drift chambers
and scintillation counters all ready
at the moment God or I light the match.

While I am not sure that this world,
in all its ecstasy of birth and pain and violent destruction,
can be adequately described
by partial differential equations,
still I find a certain honesty, peace and acceptance here
I don't find in any church. Now the warble of this bird
setting up his own experiment
reminds me how grateful I am to be here,
how grateful I am to go.

Now I reach the door, turn
and say *Good night* to my feathered colleagues,
who must know what they're doing as well as I do,
and step out into the brisk night,
the ocean of welcoming stars.

Wauna

I have spent years of my life
working to improve
the measurement of moisture in paper.
This week I am sent
to the James River paper mill at Wauna.
I breathe in the odor of sulfur and woodchips,
put on my steel-toed boots, hardhat, earplugs,
carry my gas mask.

I hear the thunder of steel roll on roll,
hiss of steam,
whirr and snap of the winder,
bells and sirens, whoops and shouts.
So much music I must take time to listen,
tune my ears, catch its peculiar song.

Now at Machine 3, after a long sheet break,
they're bringing down the tail:
threading paper through the fifty yards of rolls
and across the gaps to the take-up reel.
They know they are lucky.
They could be looking for work,
or they could be soldiers,
could have gone to the Persian Gulf
and killed or been killed.
But here, down at the wet end,
they're performing the fine art
of throwing a strip of wet newsprint
across the gap
from the couche roll to the felt
that carries it through the driers,
then they run along shouting, following it to the dry end,
lift it again with roaring air from a two-inch hose
into the stack of calender rolls
that shudder and bounce;
finally again across to the reel.

They work with furious speed and concentration,
yell above the machine's thunder,
the only Black man, trying to be the fastest on the floor,
pushes the only woman out of his way,
screaming at her.
Later she tells him
he was out of control,
and they part angry.

Now the machine is lined out,
making paper on target, twenty tons per hour.
Down on the floor
some talk of salmon, or boats;
others stare as they've stared for years
at the pale walls, the steam rising,
while I listen to all that rolling steel.
And now I can hear it sing
like a slide guitar, a bass, and a lone harmonica,
sing that country western song
about *So much love gone down the river,*
Gone down the river, so long.

And I want to sing, but I don't know the words
and anyway, we are not here to sing,
we are here to keep these machines rolling,
rolling, so we can talk about boats and salmon,
rolling so we can feed our families,
rolling so we can hear this singing that seems so endless,
about *So much love gone down the river,*
So long.

1992

It's Better to Be Depressed Than Watch TV

At each end of the open sky
is another airport,
at the end of the endless highway
another hotel. And at the end of this day
in which nothing will wait
silence awaits me.

But I don't need to be
a servant of silence
as long as there's *Free TV In Rooms*
with remote control and twenty-two channels.
I click them by, one by one.

These shows are about as much fun
as work. I might as well
head back to the mill
and watch the paper roll by.

Never mind, darken the screen.
The light shrinks, flies to infinity
and leaves me here.

It is
better to be depressed,
to be here in this strange room, lie
in my own strangeness
as quiet as the air
and watch the stars sink
one by one
behind the trees.

The Broke Pit

Way down at the dry end of the paper machine,
right under where the paper rolls onto the take-up reel,
there is a blender as large as a house:
an opening in the concrete floor
twenty feet long and as wide as a man is tall,
and beneath the floor, sloping walls
down to a blade as big and fast
as a ship's, and water pouring in
to soften, cut and beat the *broke*, the reject paper,
down to a slurry of fiber and water,
then a screen and pipe to carry it back
to the wet end, feed it back in. Nothing wasted.

You have to respect it, keep your distance
when a reel of broke
unrolls into that pit;
don't let it trip you, drag you in;
when you feed broke into that maw,
don't touch it with anything but a pole.
And when you shove scraps in,
go easy, keep your balance,
don't let it take you.

You have to think fast when someone disappears,
whether he was careless or even believed he
was broke, reject, scrap, unfit for anything but recycle
to blend into the silence of someone's morning news.

"He was right there!"
the backtender says. No one was watching;
now they look everywhere;
down there the slurry has a pinkish tinge.

They shut it off, his bones already ground,
starting their way down the pipe toward the wet end.

They shut the whole machine down.

The thundering hundred-odd
motors and steel rolls
slowly grind to a stop.
And for one minute of ungodly silence
they stand and think
about the funny way he smiled,
a joke he told,
the last time they went hunting turkey;
they think about falling,
they think if only
they could have held him.

I Tire

of this world sometimes,
think I have bloodied my head
on enough stone walls,
begin to look for God's green pasture
where I can lie down.

Then I tell myself again
about the bacteria
whose only food is stone,
who break it down into soil,
have been at it for three billion years,
are everywhere,
miles underground by now, who
have everything they need.

The Good Ol' Days

Heading into Pineville I could catch the rotten egg smell about a mile before the paper mill. That smell would permeate everything, even a book, for months, and you can't wash a book.

The guys who ran the paper machine were a friendly sort. Out on the floor by the roaring machine, in order to get someone's attention, one would grab the other guy's crotch, then lean on his shoulder to yell in his ear.

Then there was Oly. On my first trip I went with a Black colleague. Oly asked me, "What tribe is *he* from?" I replied, "The American tribe. Why? What tribe are *you* from?" But he didn't pay me any mind.

Once I was standing in the Control Room typing at the Intelligent Data Terminal and Oly, who was sitting next to me, touched my crotch, not to get my attention, just to check me out like a dog sniffing another's behind. I turned out of reach, wanted to throttle him while delivering a lecture on civilized behavior, finished my three lines of code very carefully so as not to crash the system, and left for the day. The next day the foreman said, "Oly is not from the best of families."

Then there was the wedding ritual. The day before Billy's wedding he walked into the Control Room and the foreman blocked the door behind him. Three others came for Billy, but he had been a halfback and he crouched and dove with his arms over his belt like he had just been given the handoff. They tackled him onto the concrete floor, but he kicked and scrambled through them behind the control console. They had him cornered, but he charged and smashed two of them against a wall and the others got out of his way. Even the foreman got out of his way and didn't ask him where he was going as he headed out to the parking lot.

Oly told me about the can of blue paint and how they used to blueball grooms in the good ol' days. Now the mill manager had hired a woman to work on the machine floor, and more Blacks, and more engineers who were starting to tell them how to run the paper machine. The good ol' days of this tribe had just about run out.

The Throat of the Sky

We took Jake's car. It's an old Jeep fixed up with the steering
wheel in the middle controlling all four wheels and a seat that
swivels around so he can drive in any direction. Bob and I sat
in the back seat, whatever that means. Pretty soon all we
could see was scattered scrub on dry earth. Jake turned off
the road and started up this hill going faster and faster. Sure
enough, pretty soon we were airborne and climbing way
above the landscape. We spotted an opening in the clouds, so
we headed straight for it. Jake told us they call it *The Throat
of the Sky*. When we got there we pulled right into the parking
lot of the Poker Hall. Jake warned me that they are a rough
bunch in there. You just go in, don't say any more than you
have to, and play honest, guns-on-top-of-the-table poker.
Jake and Bob got into a game right away. I headed for the
piano and played all afternoon. The games were so good, they
didn't hear a note I played. And I didn't win or lose a penny.
None of us know the way to Heaven, but I suppose Jake is
right—there's a weakness in my character: I'll never win at
poker and won't make it to Heaven. On the other hand, there
should be room for someone to play piano.

Fragile Goods

When you stack cardboard boxes
full of fragile goods, you don't want
the weight of the load above
to crush the box on the bottom. So
I arrive at the ninth
paper mill with my company's
Strength Sensor (an invention for which
I take some credit
and a lot of blame) designed
to measure the strength of paper instantly
while it's still rolling on the machine
and thus to predict the strength
of that bottom box, every box
in the stack.

I say the ninth mill
because I and the *Strength Sensor*
have been booted out of eight
so far, because it didn't quite
work. Still, my job
is to tweak the hardware just right
and wow them with statistics
which show that now it does.

After a week of excursions
into five of the seven levels
of Hell, I've got it purring along
sweetly across the twenty-foot-wide
sheet on the paper machine, spitting out
numbers, and this makes me happy, because I
am a numbers kind of guy.

Just one little thing troubles me:
One of the paper testers in the Lab
sticks out his chin and looks at me
while another carefully explains,

All the boys out by the paper machine
carry knives like this one. They easily cut
through ninety-pound board and you
better make sure no one catches you
on the back side of the machine.

For some reason,
I feel a bit misunderstood,
so I head out of the Lab
and take a brief but refreshing dip
into self-pity and despair. Then I think
and figure they expect me
to reach the airport, face still white,
before they can stop laughing. And
I have to admire
the way he intimates that *somebody*
just might kill me, but *he*
is on *my* side. Since the second is a lie,
maybe the first
is, too. In any case, a well-crafted lie
reveals intelligence, which we all need
to survive, and I, too, am now thinking
deeply about survival.

So I drop in
on their boss, tell him,
    Maybe they think
    our sensor will replace them,
    take away their jobs, but
    we both know, don't we,
    our goal is closing the loop,
    controlling strength
    and improving quality to make
    stronger boxes, isn't it? That's where
    the big bucks are.

Understand, this is not part
of my job description;
who am I to tell them
how to run their mill? But I can't wait
for our smooth-talking salesman;
my sensor could be mysteriously
damaged as at the last mill
and my skin is more delicate
than ninety-pound board.

Luckily he says,
        *Yes, of course; I'll talk
        to the boys.*

I give him a couple of hours, then wander
into the Lab and chat a bit with that fellow
with the overgrown utility knife. He tells me
how committed he is to quality, happy
to be part of the team, asks me
if I like to fish.

Once again
I admire his intelligence, see
already we have closed one loop,
am hoping now
we can keep our focus on the fragile
goods, since we both know
the bottom of the stack is one place
no one wants
or ought
to be.

Morning Ghazal

I wake at six AM hungry to know what life is.
By eight, I need to know how to cope.

Rumor has it we aren't created by God,
but by untrained amateurs who mean well.

If all my emotional blocks were laid end to end,
they would lead to a new life.

I know it is not foggy everywhere,
just everywhere I can see.

Everything I do, I do of free will.
Now, if only I could get a handle on my will.

How long can my body go on taking such a beating,
so my spirit can have what it needs?

Oh Len, if only you weren't such a slave to duty!
Oops, there I go again, talking into one of my deaf ears.

Monday Morning

Back at work,
Monday morning,
nine o'clock,
most frequent hour of death
for men.

I return to the task
others have called
impossible, while I
have remained ever eager,
have played
the superhuman.

My body has come
to resent this. Pains
pierce my legs;
I can't sit here
any longer.

Perhaps it is not too late
to stand up
and walk out of here,
this place I have even called
a kind of home. Perhaps
it is not too late
to make a home
in this body.

You Are the Center of the Universe

and so am I
and so is Steve,
here on the sidewalk
by the River St. garage
wearing earphones,
bopping and grooving half the day,

and so is another I've seen
commuting on the glistening river
of hypertension. Stopped at a light,
his truck rocks as he
gyres, and I suspect,
gimbles, too, to seventies disco.

How do I know this—
that you
are the center of the universe?

Galileo Galilei,

who bopped all night
with his telescope
and proved
the Sun does not revolve around
the Church Fathers
for which they kindly
sentenced him to life at home
so he could think and pray about this
a little longer.

And Einstein,

whose grooving
involved differential equations. He
said it right there in his
Principle of General Relativity—
All yardsticks, all frames of reference,
are equivalent.

This means that you,
in your frame,
are free
to bop and groove
in your own space and time,
with telescopes or equations,
however you please,
and if someone else,
perhaps a Church Father,
in his frame
doesn't like it,
well,
he is also free.

And every time
one of us is born, hey,
time leaps up and begins again,
fresh and totally new,
yet strangely like before.

But even that's not enough—
we are also
the *axis mundi,*
the cosmic tree
on the cosmic mountain.
Every moment is
the moment of creation, each
of our bodies
is the temple of all that is holy, and—
here is the scary part—we
have to run our own lives.

Now Steve is revolving
in slow motion
to the jive of a talk show,
so his *thoughts*
don't come apart, he tells me

while you and I and Steve, along with
the Church Fathers and all our mothers, sail
on this Earth around the Sun, wing
around the Milky Way
and fly from all other galaxies
at ever-increasing speed, which
I surely could not stand
if I were not firmly
at the center of the universe.

Excerpt from the Obituary of a Postmodernist Critic

For the history of science, the 20ᵗʰ Century has nothing of value.
    —A postmodern critic

The personal lyric is dead.
    —A postmodern poet

His life's work is based on the radical theory which holds that all language and literature, even contracts and science, are merely social constructs of texts which refer only to themselves, not to extratextual reality, and thus can only be understood via their deconstruction. His final and most influential work, *The Language Is Broken*, is an explication of his breakthrough insight that texts of deconstruction also refer only to themselves and thus have no value except through their deconstruction. The book consists of 397 one-page essays. The first takes up the deconstruction of the book's title. Each succeeding essay takes up the deconstruction of the one before. It is a mark of the purity and honesty of this work that each essay is broken off in order to immediately proceed with its deconstruction, and thus consists of only the word "The."

Another postmodern critic hailed the book as "one brilliant insight after another." One prominent detractor also gave it a positive review, saying, "In comparison to his previous works, this one attains a startling clarity and a remarkable, spare lyricism. The entire work may be seen as a unified and universal metaphor for the deconstructionist impulse. I look forward to its sequel." Here the reviewer refers to the tragically incomplete status of the project, which was interrupted when the author was felled by an anal obstruction. On the death certificate, the cause of death is listed as "suffocation."

His tombstone will be engraved with another of his widely praised insights, "Death is a social construct."

The Redwood Tree and I

Knowledge mitigates loneliness.
— Albert Einstein

The redwood tree in Ken and Coco's yard
is larger than you or I will ever be.
I wonder if it feels alone; the tallest tree around
for a hundred yards, it must take on
the full brunt of the winds that come
howling out of the north in winter.

Once in my student days I sat down
at a kitchen table in Berkeley
and, with the book closed,
calculated the spectral lines of hydrogen,
told myself, *These are lines in the thumbprint
of God*, as if to say
God is invisible
yet seen everywhere, in
each atom.

And then I said, *These
are the spectral lines of hydrogen,* meaning
what I said before was not
a testable hypothesis.

I go back and forth
between these two energies
on the tiniest current of air,
like the redwood tree.
But on any day,
when I understand
one small piece
of this world,
I, too, feel less alone.
In that moment
these two energies
are one.

Ghazal of a Physicist

In grad school I would get drunk—drunk on equations.
All along the hedgerow, the wind blew leaves in waves of
    equations.

In our yard the song of the mockingbird
sounds a lot like Schrödinger's Equation.

I still search for a word that is not broken,
still find the solace of equations.

We do it on a tabletop or far out in space,
anywhere so we can make more little equations.

When my wife can't sleep, she asks me to read to her
just one or two of her favorite equations.

Don't get me wrong—I'm no reductionist.
The touch of skin on skin is beyond any equation.

Len says, In *The Book of Names,* every word from the human tongue
is a name of God, and so is every equation.

Animal Is Spiritual

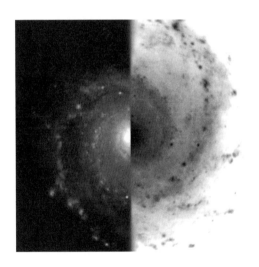

Ghazal with Black Hat

The invisible is wrapped in light, he says, with a whoosh of the Black Hat.
Or perhaps it's in here, he thinks, peering into the Black Hat.

Once upon a time when time was still sleeping,
all that now is or could ever be was asleep inside the Black Hat.

I believe in the cape and gloves, the rabbit and the wand.
There is no hat but the Black Hat.

He doesn't tell his mother. How
could he ever explain to her the Black Hat?

Oh, strange universe almost all dark matter, dark energy—
the hatter's metaphor for his own Black Hat.

Each of us is a tiny god, deciding what
to drop into, what to pull out of, the Black Hat.

The waitress thought she was in love with him.
She was in love with the Black Hat.

Every night, Freud's Unconscious and Heisenberg's Uncertainty
dine on black caviar at our expense at the oh-so-chic *Black Hat.*

We are tiny glints of light in a greater dark
within a greater yet Black Hat.

Len keeps on trying to make sense of this world.
He wouldn't have a prayer without the Black Hat.

Animal Is Spiritual

she calls out in a loud bark
from her doorstep as she sees me walk her way,
still halfway up the block. It's Nika,
the German Shepherd
who greets and licks everyone,
her slow, arthritic walk
and coat worn bare
to the black skin of her back, sign
of the sloughing off of the flesh.
I try to understand
what she means by this.

   Animal is Spiritual,
she barks again and again, and as I approach
she walks out to the street,
does not look for traffic,
crosses to my side and waits for me.

She nuzzles my pant leg, I pet her and say,
   You have a point—
   the survival advantage of softened interpersonal boundaries
   among kin in social animals could well drive a pleasure response
   that might be conditioned by the touch of a hand, the nave of a
   church, or a voice howling a hymn to the moon.
She licks my cool hand with her warm tongue.

   But surely you would admit,
I go on,
   the Animal embraces more
   than the Spiritual and the Spiritual may well embrace more
   than the Animal.

She looks up at me as if I have lost my mind.
I can read it in her eyes: *Animal is Spiritual.*

But then, what can I expect of anyone
with the limited symbolic capacity
of a *Canis familiaris?*
And I am embarrassed
to have even talked with her.

I take her by the collar back to her doormat,
tell her to be a good
spiritual dog and stay on her
side of the street. I go on with my walk.

At the end of the block I turn to see
a truck and a car stop and she
in the middle of the road,
as if she does not care
if she lives or dies. The drivers gesture,
but she pays them no mind. She just looks at me
with those eyes again—I,
another animal, a fifty-eight-year-old biped,
in the middle of the street, yelling,
    Oh saint among dogs,
    please get out of the road!

I, who still don't know what
Animal is, what
Spiritual is.

Screak

Morning is a door flung open
and a young man with earphones
wrestling his bike out into the day—
his bulbous forehead, squinting eyes,
craggy cheeks and chin, his dangling cigarette.

As I walk by I say *Hello*
and he looks me in the eyes,
cries out a clatter of broken sound.

Only once does he offer human words:
Can you fix my bike?
he asks, then disappears.
On the step I find a wrench,
tighten the bolt
so the seat does not swing free,
call in the open door,
I fixed your bike; it's OK now.
I hear only the inexplicable silence
and go on my way.

Once my wife says
Good morning, and he
drops his bike,
falls to his knees
to help her weed. She
has to tell him,
Thank you, but
you mustn't be late for work.

Still, his cry is what names him:
Day after day,
I listen
as he rolls down the hill,
the mourning doves
scattering in his path.
He stands up on his bike,
lets out a screak
like the hawk
springing from his perch
high in the Monterey pine,
falling in the morning air.

On the Nature of Things

The squawking crow
flies down from the redwood tree
to tell me
he is not a crow.

Not bird, not passerine bird
of the family *Corvidae,*
nor mind nor body
nor thing.

And not a crow.

In fact, he says,
he hasn't even been
discovered yet.

When I was young I dreamt
I climbed marble stairs
toward the room that held
The Book of What Each Thing Is.
Golden light poured down those stairs
from a room so high
I could never see it.

From that book
I would learn
what is *crow*
what is *redwood,*
what am I.

Crow tells me
the black of his wings
is deeper than any book.

Friends, there are hours
I have no greater grief,
no greater joy.

I will never know
what I am.

Crow
flies down often
to tell me so.

Nail Clippings Are Rich in Nitrogen

The soul resides in our nails,
the ancients said. I
wait till mine are too long,
then clip, file and toss
the clippings in the compost.

My nails are thick and strong,
perfect for using as a screwdriver
or scratching until I bleed.

Pink and smooth
with white moons,
they are brothers
to claws and hooves.

These parts trimmed off
will come back
in sweet peas and tangerines.

Like the ancients, I know
when you no longer
find me in this world,
my nails
will keep on
growing.

Let's Take the Mind, for Instance

No, let's start with this roll of fence wire
lying on its side
on the deck. Brown with rust,
up close
it's the work of an Impressionist, glops
of soil streaked along one half, the rust
wormed through these blobs to tint them
tones of grey and brown and orange. There is
no painter, only one roll of wire
that lay one season in the mud. See
how we stepped up close, broke it down
to find its story, then stepped back
to see the whole. So now, let's

take the mind, let's say
it is like this persimmon tree,
with leaves chartreuse of early spring,
each a window to the morning sun. Yet
none of us has ever seen a mind;
the mind is not a thing; indeed
there is no mind, only leaves and clouds,
like spring,
passing in a coastal sky, seen,
and wind, warm or brisk or damp, felt
on the skin.

No, let's say the mind is like the way
leaves turn slowly a darker green,
the opening and closing of towhee wings,
the forming of a bud.
Let's say
the mind is like spring.

The Empty Chair

The wealthy widow of a philosopher offered in his memory an endowment of a Chair in the Philosophy of Idealism. At her request each applicant was asked if only human beings should be hired rather than mere ideas in the minds of the examining committee. Each applicant agreed and then was asked to prove that he or she was more than a mere idea. After three years the widow had to give up and withdraw her endowment.

The chicken is the egg.

The widow tried again, offering a Chair in the Philosophy of Materialism. Each applicant was asked if the position should only be awarded to someone who is fundamentally different from a sack of rice, and to prove that he or she was so qualified. After three years the widow had to give up and withdraw her endowment.

Each pyramidal neuron in the human neocortex branches to nine thousand others.

She tried again, offering a Chair in the Philosophy of Consciousness. Each applicant was asked if the position should only be given to a conscious being and then was asked to prove that he or she was so qualified. After three years the widow gave up and threw a party. In her garden she and her guests took off their shoes and danced into the night.

Flies have taste buds on the soles of their feet.

The widow married a philologist who had spent forty years exposing the tacit metaphors underlying philosophical, religious and scientific theories. He was also an avid dancer, especially artful in tango.

The physical world is the body of God.

One night in the deep embrace of their dance, he told her how the failure of Western analytic thought is directly due to its failure to incorporate the Argentine tango, how all thought is a dance in which we hold the world in our arms and it holds us.

Her beauty is endless.

The newlyweds held a costume ball; each guest dressed as a metaphor. The band played, the floor lit up like a neocortex, the dancers whirled around an empty chair.

I Try Not to Shriek in the Supermarket

Sailing these aisles of the brightly-packaged dead, I think only of
    eating.
The living are bound to the dead through eating.

It was a stroke of genius to say that only humans have souls,
so we'll never meet in the afterlife all those we have eaten.

Bittersweet chocolate is the food of the gods.
On their behalf I enact daily the divine rite of its eating.

Ever since I took the round white body of Christ into my
    mouth,
I look at my fork and wonder who I am eating.

I am a kind vegetarian, with predator eyes—
evolution's design to make sure I go on eating.

In Len's last hours bring him raspberries and sweet cream.
May God take him into Her mouth with the delight of what he
    is eating.

Why Dervishes Whirl

This morning I awoke
ravenous
with a hunger
I cannot name. The wind blew
in furious grey light,
flailing the spindly arms
of the fence roses
while a gang of crows scattered,
dancing wildly.

The steady rain
mimics the rumble of distant armies
marshaled by men with an extravagant
taste for power. Soldiers
taught how to brush in boot camp
all die with clean teeth. We
who love them
shield our eyes with our hands,
weep for ourselves,
believing we weep
for them.

The whirling dervishes turn
with arms open,
the right hand up toward heaven
to receive, the left down, offering
to earth. The spiral galaxy
where we live
is driven by a team
of black horses
racing around its center,
always hungry. Only so long
as those great arms of light wheel,

will everything
not fall
toward the mouths
of the horses.

Where We Are Headed

From my dining room table
I can see a young carpenter
on a new plywood roof two stories up
lift a twelve-foot two-by-four,
balance it on one shoulder,
carry it across,
bend and place it
right on the edge.

I turn and shout
over the radio at the president,
who is telling me where
our troops are headed next:

> *Just tell me once, how many we*
> *have killed, so I can mourn them, too!*

Like so many,
I try to speak for God these days.
As near as I can tell,
God is not
overly impressed.

Outside, the succulents my wife grows
have leaves like tongues,
taste the mercy of the drops of fog,
hold it in as long as they can

while the angels,
who would save us
if only they could,
pretend they don't know us.

The Gate of Heaven is in
the Temple of Loss,
its arch
waist high.

One day we may meet there,
you, my wife and I,
the carpenter, the president.

Now is the time to practice
bending low.

April, 2002

Another One

It's true what they say: *We are all one.*
I'm just not sure we're all talking about the same one.

When I was young I knew I deserved a much greater love
than any I could give. Then I set out to find one.

You'd think we'd stop shooting when we see the piles of the
    fallen,
but no, we'd have to know each and every one.

If we just forgave God and each other, and God forgave us,
we could all shake hands, sit down and have a tall cool one.

I keep a close eye on all my illusions,
because I know how hard it is to lose one.

There are way too many things to die for.
To go on living is the best one.

Here on the skin of the Earth, Len will go on striving.
Only inside Her are we all made one.

In My Fourteenth Lifetime

A few people had way too much power. The rest of us got together and persuaded them to move to a tiny island off Tierra del Fuego.

All the Vatican's gold was melted down and shaped into teardrops. Each of us on the planet received exactly one.

The Kremlin was turned into a theme park. Hydraulic pistons lifted Stalin's corpse to sit up in his tomb and wave each time a roller coaster came by full of screaming children.

Religious fervor for a violent end of the world fell out of fashion. We recognized many forms of demonic possession.

The most exquisite instrument of torture was the clock.

There were two political parties, the *Hardasses* and the *Mushies.* Then a third emerged and took the majority, *The Tree Party.* Every time a tree was cut down, its rings were consulted for their implications for local and national policies.

Preparation of the means of war was entered into the official list of symptoms for Delusional Disorders.

By international law, each moment was proclaimed to be The Moment Of Utter Celebration And Mourning.

After work, people gathered in the forests and danced to the music of songbirds. The birds never sang out of key.

I was the same person I had been in my previous lifetimes. I was someone entirely other.

One day as we danced in the forest, I fell. There on the ground I died in the arms of my beloved, in the middle of a kiss.

Dragon Stew

O noble winged one, O carrier of spirit, O Dragon!
I sing of your lion's teeth, your flaming tongue, O Dragon.

On Chinese New Year's or Election Day, here inside
we can't see head or tail of this long dragon.

I and I and I are off to the mall
with shopping lists scrawled by lonely dragons.

It's easy to see how humans got this far:
The bigger the brain, the more room for dragons.

There at her door, I was falling. I leaned close;
she whispered, *Kiss me. Kiss my dragons.*

Science is wonderful. Now every child has a pet
dinosaur that will grow up one day into a dragon.

Literalists are eaten alive, or else they wed their moms.
Poets, too, can spiral inward, stalking dragons.

Friends ask for my recipe. I say no one
can tell you how to stew your own dragons.

Photograph of My Father at Age Ten, 1910

He stands at attention like a child soldier
in his rough-sewn pants bunched at the waist,
white shirt with sash as a tie, boots and a hat.
The sun burns bright in those eyes tucked deep
under his brows; his mouth is turned down
at the edges, an Anderson mark I also bear.
The front steps on which he stands,
the skid walkway, the grass and the hedge rose
that climbs the house
lie in the glare of the sun,
but the porch of his home is so dark
one would pause and look before stepping in.

Already he is a little man; already his father
has walked out, leaving a wife and thirteen children
three blocks from skid row;
already his mother has told him, the youngest,
to go ask his father for money,
and he has been told, *I don't know you;
go away*, and watched the door slam.

Each day the steel rod in his spine
grows, each day he learns
there are things that will haunt him
and what it means to endure,
as his mother and father did, also at age ten,
on hardtack and salt pork nine weeks
in the ship from Norway.

He will never speak a word to me
of his abandonment, but one day
after I have lived two years unwed
with the woman I love, he will tell me
I should make up my mind.
He will say, *There is something
I should tell you,* but he won't,
and I won't press him—only years later

will my niece say how,
at the breakup of her marriage,
my father called, spilled it all,
asked her to think of the children.

Today this ten-year-old
looks at me through deep-set eyes
only steps from the dark
shelter of his door and I
look hard to see
what I can rescue from this dark
and from the silence between us,
deeper now.

Listening to Antonio Mairena While the War Rages

Legendary Gypsy Flamenco singer, 1909-1983

He tells me
we are living off the blood of God.
And the dead are dancing barefoot
in the violet dust
to the *siguriyas*
from the skeletons
of guitars.

He leads me to the old well of his village,
lowers the bucket, draws it up
brimming with tears.

Ay, the blinding sun, the blinding sun of Andalucía!

He pulls the same dagger
out of his heart
seven times

and shows me the forge
in his father's blacksmith shop,
where he was apprenticed
to lightning and thunder.
He takes up the hammer
and counts out for me the cost
of one heartbeat.

He shows me silver trees
dancing on the Rio Guadalquivir,
and begs a Gypsy girl
to bring back from the dark cave
the moon she had once hung in the sky.

Ay, the blinding sun, the blinding sun of Andalucía!

I follow him down
step by step into the copper mine.
We pickaxe at the walls for centuries.

We cross the Sierra de Almijara, arrive
at the Door to the Great Silence.
We drink liquor
distilled from the bitter root of the bitter tree,
and mourn that day
when the last rose will die.

It is a mad world. What can we do? I ask.
He puts his hand on my shoulder and tells me,
We can tell what we see.
We can make beauty from pain.
We can live until we die.

Alegría

...the duende wounds. And in the healing of that wound, which never closes, lie the strange invented qualities of a man's work.
—Federico García Lorca

When we don't know anymore
what joy is, we go to see Nino,
"El Veterano," dance the Flamenco *Alegría*.
Tonight with the rolling strum of the guitars
Nino lifts his arms above his greying hair
and the singer invites us to Cádiz
where it is spring
and women have beautiful dark eyes.

But as he arcs to the center of the floor,
Nino sees only the eyes of his daughter,
dead ten years. He bows his head,
struggles to speak to her
with the language of his body.

Each step recalls
the ladder rung that snapped,
laid him out, broke his right foot.
Nino tells himself again
that if he ever stops dancing,
he will die
and he attacks the floor,
glides like a hawk
and attacks again—each step a dart
into pain, into floor, into earth
to wake the sleeping *duende*.

Back when he was a gangster *pachuco*
on the streets of San Diego,
where was the duende then?
Or when he was a wild man,
throwing knives as he danced the *Farucca*?
It had no way in.

But tonight a pair of dark wings
hovers above the stage
and just when he thinks
he cannot bear this pain any longer,
he feels himself lifted
toward heaven
while his body
goes on dancing.

Let it come, he says,
as his arms rise and he spins
with a power that is not all his own.
Let it come, as his steps
shudder with a speed
beyond control.
Let anything come,
as he explodes, a flurry of lightning bolts,
and with each pounding step
he teaches us
what joy is.

Anchor

I put my hand on my heart;
each warms the other, each knows
the warmth of two, but the hand
is the cooler partner. The hand is a door,
the heart a room I want to move into.

I feel the earth beneath me;
I listen to it breathe.
The wind ripples the leaves,
the song sparrows and towhees
scutter and peck.

While the drops of yesterday's rain
work their way down through soil
to bedrock, my body learns
to forget all those years I tried
to live anywhere but in this body.

I put my hand on my heart.
For a moment my body forgets
what it needs to forget,
and I think I could always
be this kind.

Open Ghazal

Kiss the hand and cheek, kiss the lips that open.
Kiss the eyes and tears, kiss the wounds that open.

The nuclei of our atoms are so small, we are mostly nothing.
Whoever made them, made our stone walls out of windows
    always open.

A bag too dark to see, too big to lift, too familiar to walk away
    from
deep in a thicket. God grant me strength to drag it into the
    open.

6:10, stuck on the freeway again.
Love is singing with window and throat wide open.

My friend who refused to greet the stranger in black
was brought to the surgeon, who cut his heart open.

Go ahead, I dare you, take another breath. Each one
is full of what fourteen billion years ago blew this world open.

We safecracker poets sand fingertips, pass long nights on our
    knees,
all to feel those clicks that mean the door will spring open.

Len says, I love the night sky, I adore the Milky Way:
It is the edge of Her robe. See how gently it opens.

NOTES

Page 11: "Affection for the Unknowable"; *Aquinas:* Roman Catholic theologian and philosopher Thomas Aquinas (1225-1274) proposed a cosmological proof of the existence of God in which the present must be traceable through an unbroken chain of causation to a pre-existing, eternal uncaused cause, God. We now know that many physical events, including all decays of radioactive atoms, occur at unpredictable moments without causal stimulus. While Aquinas' unbroken chain of causation was always a questionable assumption and thus not a basis for proof, 20th century science has exposed it as contrary to evidence; *quantum:* Quantum Theory describes the behavior of atomic and subatomic matter, and includes uncertainty as an essential and calculable part of the theory; *God:* Why is there anything at all? This is the greatest unknowable. This word is my personal reminder of this question and the awe it evokes in me, its capital "G" reminding me that it is the supreme unknowable. I respect that each reader will bring his or her own response to this word.

Page 12: "The Spiritual Life"; *kundalini:* in Yoga, the life force coiled at the base of the spine.

Page 29: "The Average Moment Is Two Seconds Long"; For more on the claim in this title, along with a wealth of other facts and speculations about consciousness, see *Elemental Mind* (Penguin, 1993) by Nick Herbert.

Page 34: "For the Record"; *right frontal lobe:* A study of seven patients with mental decline and shifts in personality showed brain damage in the right frontal lobe (six patients) or right temporal lobe (one patient). *Neurology*, September, 2001.

Page 35: "Night Ghazal"; The ghazal is a poetic form dating from 10th century Persia. A ghazal consists of couplets which do not follow in a narrative or thematic progression of development. Rather, each couplet could stand as a poem by itself. A refrain word or phrase is repeated at the end of each couplet and both lines of the first couplet. In the last couplet, called the signature couplet, the poet typically inserts his or her name. The traditional form also includes rhyme before the refrain and metrical lines.

Page 39: "Listen, Hephaestus"; *Hephaestus:* the Greek god of fire and the forge. He is thought to have special relevance to craftsworkers, technologists, scientists and artists; *antenna for the cosmic microwave background:* AT&T researchers accidentally discovered the radiation from the remnant shell of the Big Bang "glowing" in the microwave radio region of the electromagnetic spectrum; *Eight hundred sixty four strands of glass:* 864 optical fibers are bundled in transoceanic cables.

Page 42: "The Birds in the Bevatron"; *Bevatron:* accelerator used for research on the properties of atomic nuclei and subnuclear particles; *Rad Lab:* informal name for the Lawrence Berkeley Laboratory. No research or development work on nuclear weapons is performed there; *partial differential equations:* The equations describing the motions of astronomical objects under gravity (General Relativity) and those describing the motions of subatomic particles (Quantum Mechanics) are all partial differential equations, i.e. they include the rates of change of quantities with respect to space and/or time coordinates.

Page 44: "Wauna"; In modern paper machines a dilute mixture of wood fibers is sprayed onto the *web*—a moving woven plastic cloth which allows water to drain through but supports the forming sheet of fibers. The web then lays the sheet onto the *couche roll,* a hollow steel roll or cylinder with many fine holes, and which is evacuated by a pump, thus sucking more water from the sheet. The sheet is then transferred to the *felt*—another woven plastic cloth—for transport through the dryers. After the dryers, most kinds of paper are passed through the *calender,* a stack of heavy steel rolls, each one compressing the sheet to make it more compact, smoother and more printable. The completed paper is then rolled up onto the take-up reel.

Page 47: "The Broke Pit"; *backtender:* the person in charge of the area around the take-up reel.

Page 56: "Morning Ghazal"; The second couplet is my wording of a remark made by Robert Bly.

Page 58: "You Are the Center of the Universe"; *axis mundi:*

the "axle of the world" about which the world revolved in ancient cosmologies. It was said to enter the Earth at the center of the world, which was assumed by each nation to be its own territory. Page 61: "Excerpt from the Obituary of a Postmodernist Critic;" Disturbed by the apparent lack of intellectual rigor in postmodern critisicm, physicist Alan Sokal set out to experimentally investigate its standards of scholarship: "Would a leading North American journal of cultural studies...publish an article liberally salted with nonsense if (a) it sounded good and (b) it flattered the editors' ideological preconceptions?" In 1996 his 39-page essay "Transgressing the Boundaries: Toward a Transformative Hermeneutics of Quantum Gravity" was published in *Social Text,* a periodical "applying the latest interpretive methods to the world at large." Sokal then exposed it as a parody. A rich set of reference links to the controversy generated by this hoax can be found on Sokal's website:
http://www.physics.nyu.edu/faculty/sokal/

Page 62: "The Redwood Tree and I"; *the spectral lines of hydrogen:* hydrogen gas absorbs light at specific wavelengths which show up as dark lines when the resulting light spectrum is fanned out by a prism. The calculation of these lines via Bohr's model of the atom was an early confirmation of quantum mechanical methods.

Page 63: "Ghazal of a Physicist"; *Schrödinger's Equation:*
$$-\left(\hbar^2/2m\right)\nabla^2\Psi + V\Psi = i\hbar\,\partial\Psi/\partial t\ ;$$
reductionist: one who holds or practices reductionism, i.e., explains a complex matter in terms of a simpler one; often used disparagingly.

Page 67: "Ghazal with Black Hat"; *dark matter:* the rate of rotation of galaxies implies the existence of (gravitationally attractive) matter which is of an unknown nature and invisible to current instruments; *dark energy:* the acceleration of the expansion of the universe implies the existence of a gravitationally repulsive property of unknown nature, possibly a property of the vacuum (empty space); *Heisenberg's Uncertainty:* the uncertainty in simultaneous measurement of position and velocity or energy and time, a result of Quantum Theory.

Page 68: *"Animal Is Spiritual"; pleasure response:* reflex in which sensation of pleasure is part of a stereotypical response to a specific stimulus. If the response to the stimulus is adaptive, then evolution will select for the response, including the pleasure.

Page 76: "The Empty Chair"; *Chair:* professorship; *Philosophy of Idealism:* philosophical theory which holds that we can know only the contents of our minds; *Materialism:* the doctrine that only matter exists; *pyramidal neuron:* pyramid-shaped nerve cells; *neocortex:* outer layer of the brain, responsible for complex cognitive processes; *Philosophy of Consciousness:* attempts to create a conceptual framework in which we can understand the fact of conscious experience; *Western analytic thought:* use of formal logic and the analysis of language in order to create a formal language with which to express propositions and test their truth or falsehood. See *Philosophy in the Flesh* (Basic Books, 1999) by George Lakoff and Mark Johnson for a thorough exposition of the difficulties caused by unrecongnized metaphors in traditional Western philosophy.

Page 79: "Why Dervishes Whirl"; *spiral galaxy where we live:* there is good evidence that the center of the Milky Way is a very large black hole, a body of matter of such density and mass that nothing can escape its gravitational attraction, not even light. In fact, black holes are seen to draw in large masses of stars and dust.

Page 86: "Photograph of My Father at Age 10, 1910"; see page 99.

Page 88: "Listening to Antonio Mairena While the War Rages"; This poem is not in any sense a translation of songs sung by Antonio Mairena; *siguriya:* solemn, mournful Flamenço music and dance form; *Rio Guadalquivir:* river that runs through Córdoba and Seville; *Sierra de Almijara:* mountain range east of Málaga. Flamenco is a music and dance form of the Gypsies, now often called Roma, who came from northern India through the Middle East to Andalusia in southern Spain in a series of migrations. In 1492 Ferdinand and Isabella decreed that all who live in Spain must be Catholic, and forced the Moors, Jews and Gypsies to convert, leave Spain, hide or face the Inquisition. Flamenco evolved in this climate of persecution as the Gypsies banded together with Moors, Jews and other outcasts. It blends influences from Spanish, Jewish, Arabic and other music and dance forms. Antonio Mairena is still recognized by many as the greatest Flamenco singer. He also collected and published many songs that were on the verge of being lost.

Page 90: "Alegría"; *Alegría:* Spanish for joy, also a joyful Flamenco dance; *duende:* a Dionysian spirit which is said to possess artists at their height of creative power; *pachuco:* gangster kid; *Farucca:* manly Flamenco dance.

Page 93: "Open Ghazal"; *14 billion years ago:* the current best estimate of the age of the universe is 13.7 billion years.

Len Anderson was born and raised on the San Francisco Peninsula and received his BA and PhD in physics from the University of California, Berkeley. As a physicist he worked in experimental elementary particle physics at Berkeley and in Europe; in private industry he developed sensors for the automation of paper manufacturing. He is a winner of the Dragonfly Press Poetry Competition and the Mary Lonnberg Smith Poetry Award. He and his wife live in Santa Cruz County, California. He is a co-founder of Poetry Santa Cruz.